LETTERS TO HIGH SCHOOL
Girls

What We Wish We Had Known

KELSEY TISCHLER

Letters to High School Girls: What We Wish We Had Known

Copyright © 2025 by Kelsey Tischler

Psalm 139 Publishing

Email: ktischler23@gmail.com

ISBN: 979-8-218-54382-2

All rights reserved. No part of this publication may be reproduced, distributed, or transmitted in any form or by any means, including photocopying, recording, or other electronic or mechanical methods, without prior written permission, except in the case of brief quotations embodied in critical reviews and certain other noncommercial uses permitted by copyright law.

Unless otherwise indicated, Scripture quotations are from the Holy Bible, New International Version®, NIV®. Copyright ©1973, 1978, 1984, 2011 by Biblica, Inc.™. Used by permission. All rights reserved worldwide. www.zondervan.com The "NIV" and "New International Version" are trademarks registered in the United States Patent and Trademark Office by Biblica, Inc.™

Scripture quotations marked ESV are from The ESV® Bible (The Holy Bible, English Standard Version®), copyright © 2001 by Crossway, a publishing ministry of Good News Publishers. Used by permission. All rights reserved.

Scripture quotations marked NKJV are from the New King James Version®. Copyright © 1982 by Thomas Nelson. Used by permission. All rights reserved.

TC-TY

DEDICATION

To High School Girls

"I praise you because I am fearfully and wonderfully made; your works are wonderful, I know that full well."

PSALM 139:14

CONTENTS

Introduction	1
Letter #1 - Shannon	5
Letter #2 - Lily	9
Letter #3 - Cali	13
Letter #4 - Caitlyn	17
Letter #5 - Denali	19
Letter #6 - Sionna	23
Letter #7 - Hannah	27
Letter #8 - Molly	31
Letter #9 - Maria	37
Letter #10 - Julia	41
Letter #11 - Anne Shirley	43
Letter #12 - Breanne	47
Letter #13 - Sydney	51
Letter #14 - Rachel	57
Letter #15 - Em	59
Letter #16 - Erin	63
Letter #17 - Brooke	67
Letter #18 - Mia	71
Letter #19 - Macy	77
Letter #20 - Mackenzie	79
Letter #21 - Daniela	83

Letter #22 - Krystal	85
Letter #23 - Janine	91
Letter #24 - Emily	93
Letter #25 - Kailyn	95
Letter #26 - Julia	99
Letter #27 - Kirsten	103
Letter #28 - Ese	107
Letter #29 - Megan	111
Letter #30 - Jen	115
Letter #31 - Danielle	117
Letter #32 - Mo	121
Letter #33 - Ellie	125
Letter #34 - Emily	129
Letter #35 - Rachel	137
Letter #36 - Natalie	139
Letter #37 - Kelsey	141
Acknowledgements	143

INTRODUCTION

"What do you wish you had known your freshman year of high school?" That was the question my 14-year-old sister, Meghan, asked me one summer when I was home from college. I gave her my answer, then an idea came to mind: What if I asked some friends to write a letter to Meghan in response to that same question? I knew they would have godly wisdom to share, so I reached out, and the letters started filling my sister's mailbox.

Meghan found the words of these college-aged women to be impactful and encouraging as she entered this new season of life. A few years later, toward the end of her high school career, she told me she still read over the letters. After hearing that, God put it on my heart to compile them into this book so other high school girls could read them as well. Along with the original letters to my sister, I invited other friends of mine to write in response to the same prompt.

Slight adjustments were made so the letters would be relevant to high school girls of *all* grades, not just freshmen. Also, biblical citations were added in order to share what God says about the topic at hand. I strongly encourage you to read the Scripture references in your Bible! The Word of God is a far better resource and teacher than these letters (2 Timothy 3:16–17; Hebrews 4:12). When you

Introduction

look up a specific reference, read the verses before and after it to understand what is going on in that full section of Scripture. Understanding the context helps us to properly interpret the Bible.

It is important to say that these letters were written to my sister with the understanding that she is a Christian. Some of the statements and encouragements made are only true for those who have trusted in Jesus as their Lord and Savior. This is the *most* important decision of your life! Let me explain why...

God is completely perfect and sinless. On the other hand, we are all sinners who have fallen short of the glory of God (Romans 3:23). Because of this, we are not able to be in a right relationship with Him here on earth or when we die (Isaiah 59:2). This means we will be separated from God for all eternity, away from heaven. But there is hope! God loved us so much that He made a way for us to be in a relationship with Him. He did this by sending to earth His Son, Jesus Christ, as a sacrifice for us (Romans 5:6–8). After 33 years, Jesus gave up His life by being crucified on a cross, paying the price for our sins, and satisfying the wrath of God that we deserved. They buried Jesus, but after three days He rose from the grave in power, defeating the hold of sin (Mark 16:4–6)!

In doing this, Christ fulfilled what was foreshadowed hundreds of years earlier in the Old Testament book of Isaiah: "He was pierced for our transgressions, he was crushed for our iniquities; the punishment that brought us peace was on him, and by his wounds we are healed" (Isaiah 53:5). In the New Testament, Scripture states that if you repent of your sins and "declare with your mouth, 'Jesus is Lord,' and believe in your heart that God raised him from the dead, you will be saved" (Romans 10:9). By God's grace, when you do this, you become a child of God and have the amazing privilege of being in a right relationship with Him here on earth and for eternity (John 1:12–13). Praise the Lord! As a child of God, it is important to get connected to a local Bible-believing church so you can be encouraged, be held accountable, and grow in your knowledge of the Lord within the family of believers.

Jesus has changed my life, and He has the power to change yours as well, no matter where you are or what you have done. Christ seeks and saves the lost (Luke 19:10)! In these letters, you will read more about Jesus. I hope the words of these young women are a source of guidance to you as they were for my sister. Our high school years were filled with moments of joy and trials, but through it all, we learned a few things that we want to pass on to you. So here you have it; this is what we wish we had known...

In Christ,

Kelsey

"Do not conform to the pattern of this world, but be transformed by the renewing of your mind. Then you will be able to test and approve what God's will is—his good, pleasing and perfect will."

ROMANS 12:2

LETTER #1

Dear Meghan,

I hope and pray high school is going well! Here are some thoughts I'd like to share with you—lessons I've learned and advice I have to offer as someone who's been in your shoes not too long ago.

When I was in high school, I was very concerned with my appearance and other people's opinions of me, so much so that I let those things define me. I wanted others to accept me and I thought I could make sure that happened by being likable and maintaining a perfect exterior. I tried to be nice to everyone and be perfect in how I looked and how I acted. That wore me out. I was putting my self-worth in my appearance and what others thought of me. I struggled with eating and body image because I was trying to achieve what I thought was the "perfect body." I found myself caught in an unhealthy cycle of not eating enough, overeating, beating myself up for it, and repeating that all over again. During that time, I thought it was a struggle I would have to deal with for the rest of my life. Little did I know though, the Lord had much better plans for me, plans to give me freedom.

Letter #1

By the grace of God, I have learned my self-worth does not come from my appearance or what others think of me. Instead, my worth comes from God alone. He says I am loved and wonderfully made, and He says that about you too (Psalm 36:7; Psalm 139:14). Along the way, I have realized true beauty comes from within. A verse I have memorized and say to myself every so often is 1 Samuel 16:7 (NKJV), "man looks at the outward appearance, but the Lord looks at the heart." It is true the world we live in focuses on the outward appearance. It is also true though, the Lord's opinion holds more value than any human's.

The thing is, people's opinions of you can change from day to day. They judge you based on your performance or appearance, which fluctuates often. So, if you put your worth in what others think of you, you're setting yourself up for a rocky ride full of ups and downs. But if you find your worth in what God thinks, who is the same yesterday, today, and forever, you can live with eternal joy and freedom (Hebrews 13:8).

The best way to continually focus on what God thinks of us is by filling our minds with His truth, which means reading and memorizing His Word (John 17:17). What we fill ourselves with enters our hearts and minds, shaping us into who we become. So if we want to become more like Christ, we should renew our minds and fill ourselves with His Word (Romans 12:2). Continually doing this will lead to experiencing peace and joy that is greater than we can understand.

So my advice to you, Meghan, is to draw near to God. Fill your mind and heart with His truth, and find your worth in what

He says about you. You have been created uniquely and beautifully. God's love for you is greater than you can ever understand (Ephesians 3:16–19). He is always with you and always faithful (Psalm 33:4; Isaiah 41:10). It is evident just from spending a few minutes with you that He has already given you the gift of His joy. Continue to share that joy and to be a light for Christ.

Love and prayers,

Shannon

"The thief comes only to steal and kill and destroy; I have come that they may have life, and have it to the full."

JOHN 10:10

LETTER #2

Dear Meghan,

Looking back on high school, there are two specific things I wish I had done differently: 1) Get connected to Christian community and 2) Be more cautious about social media usage.

I liked going to youth group at my church freshman year. A big reason for that was I enjoyed hanging out with my brothers and their friends. It was just a fun social time. I also was in a girls' small group. I don't want to admit it, but to be honest, I judged a lot of the girls there. I would think, "She's weird...I don't relate to her." I really regret this attitude. I cut these relationships off because the girls were not "popular" and "cool" like others I knew. This selfish and prideful attitude led to me not having Christian community. Looking back, it was a huge missed opportunity and greatly hindered my faith development. I encourage you to not fall into this trap like I did. Invest deeply in Christian community (Hebrews 10:24–25). Pour into others and have others pour into you. Please, when it comes to friends, don't focus on all the surface-level things. Seek out girls who can hold you accountable, encourage you in the Word, and be an ear to listen (1 Thessalonians 5:11).

Letter #2

Social media is something I spent way too much time on in high school. It definitely had a negative impact on me. I wasted too many nights isolating myself from my family because I was scrolling on my phone, trying to live my life vicariously through other girls. I wish I had left my room, put down my phone, and spent time with family! What pulled me to social media was it seemed to help numb the emotional pain I was feeling. In reality, it didn't take away the pain, it actually caused more. Without realizing it, scrolling caused me to constantly compare myself to others and care about their opinions way too much. This led to me being discontent with my body and developing very bad body image issues. So please, be mindful of how you are spending your time and the impact social media is having on you. It can make you believe that if you look a certain way, have a certain following, or get so many likes, you are "truly living." This is such a lie! Full life and true contentment can be found in Christ alone (John 10:10)! I love the verse from Proverbs 19:23, "The fear of the LORD leads to life; then one rests content, untouched by trouble."

Lily

"Since, then, you have been raised with Christ, set your hearts on things above, where Christ is, seated at the right hand of God. Set your minds on things above, not on earthly things."

COLOSSIANS 3:1–2

LETTER #3

To the girl in high school,

Being 20 years old now, I feel far removed from my high school self...but by most standards of time, it was not that long ago! I have grown in basically every aspect of my life since then. So, I would tell my high school self quite a few things.

Honestly, the first thing I would tell myself is to stop obsessing over boys. In high school, I would constantly imagine myself sitting next to a cute guy, and he would strike up a conversation with me. And then (still in my head) one thing would lead to another, we would start liking each other, we would date...and then I would be happy! I would literally go through this scenario with every cute boy in any one of my classes at a given moment. Thoughts of this boy would consume my mind. After every glance or conversation I would get my hopes up, and then they would come crashing down. I quickly realized that he wasn't on the same page as my coming-of-age movie fairytale that I had conjured up in my mind. So, I would've saved myself a lot of bad moods and heartbreak if I had just focused my mind on God, not worldly stuff (Colossians 3:1–2). In high school, you have so many things on your plate! Take it all in, whether it be training for your sport, making new friends, taking classes, etc. Enjoy the process instead of worrying about what boys you should like and what boys might like you. Your purpose is absolutely not rooted in another human being. It is rooted in Jesus Christ.

On a similar note, I wish I hadn't let my self-worth depend on external validation. I would want my high school self to know how cool she was, whether she was invited to parties or not. I would say to her, "The plan of your life belongs to God and He works all things for the good of those who love Him" (Romans 8:28).

Above all, I would say to my high school self to never take a single moment for granted. Every dance, every football game, every hangout, every Portillo's run, every sunset, every family dinner!!! Make the most of it because you never know what is going to happen in the future. The last third of my senior year was canceled due to the onset of the COVID-19 pandemic, and all of it halted to a stop. When news of the pandemic spread on March 13, 2020, I remember walking to third-period Spanish class thinking, "I may never walk through these halls again." And I was right. It still blows my mind how everything changed in the blink of an eye. If it happened once, it can happen again. So, just take everything day by day, not getting too caught up in plans for the future. High school is about so much more than just academics. It is about the entire experience, the memories, and the life lessons.

Cali

"Then Jesus said to his disciples: 'Therefore I tell you, do not worry about your life, what you will eat; or about your body, what you will wear. For life is more than food, and the body more than clothes.'"

LUKE 12:22-23

LETTER #4

Dear Meghan,

If I could go back in time and talk to my high school self, there is a lot I would want to say to her. I'd want her to fully blend her makeup. I'd want her to know black and navy do not match. I'd want her to stop biting her nails in class. I'd want her to take AP Literature. I'd want her to only wash her hair every other day and straighten her hair every morning. I'd want her to do more strength training, and I'd want her to pick out her outfits the night before.

Most importantly, I would want her to know that none of that actually mattered.

Caitlyn

"You see, at just the right time, when we were still powerless, Christ died for the ungodly. Very rarely will anyone die for a righteous person, though for a good person someone might possibly dare to die. But God demonstrates his own love for us in this: While we were still sinners, Christ died for us."

ROMANS 5:6–8

LETTER #5

Meghan,

High school can be a very competitive environment. There are grades, achievements, rankings, extracurricular accomplishments, and even the well-known (but unspoken) popularity contests. This is a time when you may develop a fear of failure. The world will tell you to cope with this pressure and stress through "self-love." Society will encourage daily affirmations and positive phrases like, "You are enough!" "Love yourself!" This doesn't get at the heart of the issue though. True freedom from this pressure and stress is found in Jesus.

Although I grew up going to church and being told all the different things the Bible said, it took me until I was a full-grown adult to really dive into reading it for myself. Before I started really reading it, sometimes the Bible felt like a test. In my head it was full of all these things I could fail at, and that was very daunting to me. The Bible, in reality, is the opposite of that. Do not be scared to read it! It is an incredible book, fully inspired by God (2 Timothy 3:16–17). In its pages you'll see that you are loved unconditionally by a very great God who sent His Son to earth to pay the price for your sins (Romans 5:6–8). God desires that we flourish under Him.

We won't ever be perfect when it comes to grades, popularity, rankings, etc., nor will we ever be perfect when it comes to measuring up to God's standard of being in relationship with Him. But God loved us so much that He made a way for us to be in a right relationship with Him through sending His Son, Jesus, to pay the price on the cross—a price we could never pay ourselves (Titus 3:4–7). When we repent of our sins and accept Him as our Savior we are privileged to be called a daughter of God…that is our greatest and truest identity (1 John 3:1). In this, we have freedom from all the overwhelming pressures to perform and succeed at the things in this world. This is great news! Your identity and worth are in Jesus, not your accomplishments. So you can go out and give 100% effort, having no fear of failure because your value isn't in your performance. No matter how great the success or how humiliating the failure, your worth to God is unchanging. You are already loved and chosen by Him.

While it is important to always strive to do the right things, inevitably there are going to be times in your life when you mess up and sin (Romans 3:23). When you do sin, it is easy to want to tuck it under the rug and say, "I'm not going to tell anyone because I won't ever do this again." This is a dangerous slope! Sinful secrets fester in the darkness. It's always best to bring these sins into the light. Confess to God and then to a trusted Christian friend, sibling, parent, or mentor so they can pray for you and walk alongside you in repentance (James 5:16). You will never mess up so badly that God will not forgive you after you make a sincere confession and turn away from your sin (1 John 1:9).

God's way of working things out in our lives may look different than what we think is best. You can always trust that His ways are higher than our own (Isaiah 55:8-9). For example, I really wanted to go to college and be a D1 athlete. This was my dream and I thought I would finally have "made it" if I could land a spot on a team. I met with multiple D1 coaches and prayed a lot about it. I did not land a big enough scholarship though, and I ended up going to a D3 school instead. I was devastated. I thought, "Maybe if I work super hard, I can transfer out after my freshman year on scholarship." But, I actually ended up getting injured in the fall season of my freshman year and could not play my sport that season, forcing me to stay at the D3 school. When I finally embraced being at that school, God worked wonders in my life. I learned so much, had a ton of fun, and made lifelong best friends who have helped me through so many situations in my life. Looking back, I cannot imagine trading all these memories, people, and experiences for a few comments like, "Wow! You are going to a D1 school!" from people who wouldn't think twice about it after the conversation ends. Although I thought going to a D1 school would be the best thing at the time, God knew I needed to be at the D3 school to grow in different ways and experience all the wonderful things He had in store. I am so thankful that I was not in control of my future and He was!

Denali

"I am the good shepherd; I know my sheep and my sheep know me—just as the Father knows me and I know the Father—and I lay down my life for the sheep."

JOHN 10:14–15

LETTER #6

Dear High School Self,

Life will bring lots of different seasons. Some of them will be incredible and unforgettable, others will be harder than you think you can handle. God will be the Good Shepherd to carry you through them all (John 10:11–15). Continue to cultivate habits that will last through the ups and downs—habits of spending time in God's Word, going to church, developing deep friendships, etc. In the good seasons, remember to keep growing. In the hard seasons, remember to look back on God's faithfulness.

Love freely and forgive often, as Christ does. You will be surprised how often something that feels big in a friendship is just a misunderstanding or lack of communication. It is not worth walking away when perhaps all that is needed is a little humility and an honest conversation. The friends that last through these tough moments are the ones worth keeping!

Always fight for your family. That doesn't mean you have to be close to them physically or that your relationship has to look picture-perfect, but keep praying and striving to love the people

Letter #6

God has put closest to you. It will pay off in dividends down the road.

Stand up for what you believe! It is surprisingly easy to compromise what you believe for the sake of a friend or boy—and even easier to conceal it from others. If your conscience is unsure, this is a red flag! Have close friends in your life that you genuinely admire, who you can be completely open with. You will find life to be much sweeter as you live in God's light instead of the darkness (1 John 1:5–7).

There are many things I could say to you, but oftentimes lessons are learned through experience. God has a way of bringing us into situations that will shape us into the person He wants us to become. So, keep your eyes open for those moments and try to learn what He has to teach you. Enjoy the adventure!

Sionna

"And let us consider how we may spur one another on toward love and good deeds, not giving up meeting together, as some are in the habit of doing, but encouraging one another—and all the more as you see the Day approaching."

HEBREWS 10:24–25

LETTER #7

To the girl in high school,

I have been in your shoes, and I know there are probably some quiet battles you are facing. There are moments of high school that are awkward and scary. It can feel like trying to get noticed in a crowd full of tall people. You want to be seen by the good-looking guys or acknowledged by the "popular girl" friend group. You want to have nice clothes like they do or be able to wear makeup that doesn't even look like you are wearing makeup. It's a comparison battle, and unfortunately, I got pulled into the fight during high school.

I was the quiet girl on the soccer team, the one everyone overlooked, and people treated me accordingly. It was so hard to go day by day losing the comparison battle I was fighting. Thoughts would run through my mind, "Why can't I pull off the outfits they do? Why don't guys talk to me like they talk to them? Why do they get so many likes on social media?" Looking back, all these struggles were rooted in insecurity and fear of being rejected. However, it didn't last all four years for me. I made the decision to get more involved in my church's youth group and started attending Young Life. It was there I came to realize the truth…not being popular isn't the end of the world. In God's kindness, He put fellow believers in my life who loved me like Christ. They were so helpful as I fought the high school comparison battle. If you are blessed to have these kinds of people in your life, hold on to them!

Hannah

"See what great love the Father has lavished on us that we should be called children of God! And that is what we are!"

1 JOHN 3:1

LETTER #8

Dear Meghan,

I remember my first day of high school like it was yesterday: the nerves, the excitement, the possibilities, the fear. I was told high school was a time to try on different identities, dip my toes into a number of waters, and discover who I truly was by the end.

I took this advice to heart, and throughout high school I explored widely. In my first year, I joined the creative writing, bioethics, and sports leadership clubs. I spent time with jocks who reeked of sweat masked only partly by Axe, with popular girls who spoke incessantly of "bikini-ready bodies" and fad diets, and with self-proclaimed nerds who flaunted their GPAs like first-time mothers do their newborn babies. I wore ruffled skirts and satin bows to class on some days and basketball shorts with Nike Elites on others. And yet, nothing seemed to click. High school felt like a bubble floating out in front of me, like I could see into it but was not actually a part of it. No matter how desperately I chased after them, belonging and acceptance seemed perpetually determined to elude me, disappearing into the night without a trace.

Letter #8

In my second year of high school, I transferred schools. On day one I met a boy who I will refer to as Sam. Sam was intelligent, charismatic, and funny. He possessed a contagious excitement for life and an appreciation for novelty. He had a warm gaze and a sincere smile. He was cool without trying to be, and much to my surprise, he wanted to date me.

Sam was my first boyfriend. At first, we went to drive-in movie theaters and hole-in-the-wall cafés. He surprised me with flowers and good morning texts. He kissed me for the first time on the top of a mountain, and he danced with me in the rain. I loved being a girlfriend. I loved being *his* girlfriend, being seen, known, chosen, and cherished by someone. Then after about a year, things began to change. Sam suddenly wanted to spend more and more time in my room and treated my boundaries like mere recommendations. His alphabet consisted increasingly of rolled eyes, crossed arms, and irritated sighs. He stopped asking about my childhood and leaving salt-water taffy on my desk.

A couple of months later, one of my classmates told me that Sam had been seeing someone else behind my back. With that, the initial sweetness of our relationship immediately subsided and betrayal instantly took its place. I broke up with him over the phone, in between choked tears, with a teddy bear tucked in my arms. The next several months were difficult. I repeatedly caved to the temptation to check Sam and his new girlfriend's social media, and I faced ill treatment from several of his close friends.

No longer a girlfriend, grades became my primary source of validation. I poured all of my excess time and energy into school. I was a straight-A student and won awards in every subject. Perhaps this was who I was meant to be all along. Then, like my relationship with Sam, the thrill of my new identity soon wore off. It wasn't long before the frequency of my panic attacks began to increase, and I felt the pit in my stomach deepen before every test. Even though I encountered Christ for the first time in my junior year of high school, it wasn't until I got to college that I began to recognize my errors.

I had perceived high school as an opportunity to find my identity, and to do so, I had looked to the world. The reality is, I was never going to discover who I truly was in the heart of a boy or on an academic transcript. I wasn't going to find the real me in a high school club or in the company of popular girls. The one and only place where I was going to find my identity was in Christ. In Him, I am seen, known, cherished, and chosen (Psalm 139:1–4; 1 Peter 2:9). Knowing this reality changed my life. With my worth found in Jesus, I can now confidently say I know who I am. I am a daughter of the Lord Most High, and my citizenship lies in Heaven (Philippians 3:20).

For much of my life, I fell for the lies of culture. The only way I was able to renew my mind with truth was through prayer and delving into the unchanging Word of God (Isaiah 40:8; John 17:17; Romans 12:2). It is in those words I found who I am and what I am made for. The Bible is a deep enough water for us to dive into each day and learn new things about the One who created us.

As you go through high school, I encourage you to remember these truths. Yes, challenge yourself and be willing to try new things, but don't go searching for your identity in them. Regardless of your interests or social group, you are first and foremost a child of God if you have a true relationship with His Son (1 John 3:1). Embrace your relationship with Him and abide always in His love (John 15:9). I leave you with Jesus' words in John 15:5 (ESV), "I am the vine; you are the branches. Whoever abides in me and I in him, he it is that bears much fruit, for apart from me you can do nothing."

With love always, your sister and friend:

Molly

*"Know that the L*ORD *is God. It is he who made us, and we are his; we are his people, the sheep of his pasture."*

PSALM 100:3

LETTER #9

Dear Younger Me,

If I can promise you one thing, it's that it truly does all work out. The worries about the future and the fear of what's next will fade once you realize that the God who created the universe has also created a plan for you, His daughter (Genesis 1:1; John 1:3).

Because these truths exist, step into the unknown with the utmost peace and confidence in Him. Make it a point to truly enjoy every moment because they will so quickly pass by. Embrace the uncertainty, allowing yourself to take it all in rather than worrying about the future.

High school can be a harsh place. Don't take yourself too seriously. Remember God made you and you are His (Psalm 100:3). There will be pressure to stay up to date on the latest style trends, grow your social media presence, and hang out with the popular crowd. Instead of falling into this trap, trailblaze your own path. (Read: eat lunch with those eating alone, wear the shirt your mom picked out for you and appreciate her because she's truly always on your side, and spend time with your family because these are moments you'll never get back.) Years from now, no one will care if a football player didn't ask you to wear his jersey at the game or if you didn't get asked to homecoming. No one will ask how many likes you got on your social media post. No one will wonder why you weren't at that party. The moments you'll remember are the ones spent living the life you were called to live, not obsessing about what others think of you.

Lastly, you are wonderfully made (Psalm 139:14). The body you were given will do amazing things in this lifetime. You were made for more than worrying about the gap between your thighs or the way you look in a bathing suit. Always remember: Dive headfirst into your academic interests. Quality is always better than quantity in friends. Don't forget to call your grandparents. Find your Jesus people; they will hold you when you need to be held. And never miss the chance to tell someone you love them.

You've got this,

xx Maria

"Consider it pure joy, my brothers and sisters, whenever you face trials of many kinds, because you know that the testing of your faith produces perseverance. Let perseverance finish its work so that you may be mature and complete, not lacking anything."

JAMES 1:2–4

LETTER #10

Dear Meghan,

In high school, I wish I realized how short the time was. Four years feels like forever, and yet it's just a moment in the grand scheme of things. I say that not to minimize the importance of how it shapes a person, because it certainly does; however, whether it's a friendship gained or lost, recognition, awards, new opportunities, immense joy, or deep pain...it all passes in its time. God uses every moment to shape us, but He doesn't keep us in the moment forever. I would remind myself that each moment will instruct me how to better respond in the future and add to the story in the end. Above all, I would tell myself that the painful moments are used by the Lord to teach us (Romans 5:3–5; James 1:2–4). They refine and test one's character, making us who we will become in the long run.

Overall, if I could go back in time and tell my high school self something, I would say: "Dig into every moment. Drink deeply of the highs and depend on God through the lows. Journal and keep a record of everything so that you don't forget who you were and what you have become. It will encourage you one day down the road."

With love,
Julia

"Am I now trying to win the approval of human beings, or of God? Or am I trying to please people? If I were still trying to please people, I would not be a servant of Christ."

GALATIANS 1:10

LETTER #11

Dear Younger Me,

Please know people aren't as focused on you as you might think, and that is very good news...

I was selfish in high school and that made me stressed. I remember always thinking that everyone cared what I was doing. People cared what car I drove. People cared how I looked in the morning. People cared how I did on my last test, and people cared how I performed in my sport. I was always looking for ways I could hide things I was embarrassed about and would sneakily bring up my accomplishments so that other people would recognize them and be impressed. I was sure my peers were invested in what I was doing, and they were thinking about me and judging me constantly.

What I didn't know was that everyone else in my school thought the same thing about themselves. And if everyone is constantly thinking about themselves, then they *can't* always be thinking about me. In reality, no one cared or likely even *noticed* all those things I was worried about. Everyone is too concerned with thinking about their own image.

Letter #11

As I have come to realize that most people don't really even notice or care that much about what I do, I have found freedom to care less myself. I don't have to be ashamed about an embarrassing incident or try so hard to get people to recognize my accomplishments because, in reality, they probably don't care that much. It is a hard thing to relinquish your concern about other people's judgments. It is something that can never truly be perfected; however, there is freedom in the practice.

Anne Shirley

"Do not be misled: 'Bad company corrupts good character.'"

1 CORINTHIANS 15:33

LETTER #12

Dear Meghan,

High school is overwhelming and so exciting at the same time. Just in case you're a little nervous, here are some tips I wish I'd known in high school. First off, there is this societal pressure that high school is supposed to be the best four years of your life. It doesn't always turn out that way, so don't stress when you have tough days. Sometimes it's not all it's cracked up to be, and that's ok :)

Second, the less you care about what other people think of you, the happier you'll be. I know being a part of the "in crowd" seems like the most important thing in the world. I promise you though, seeking out a handful of key friends who truly understand and care about you will be so much more life-giving. As a sub-topic to that, if there needs to be alcohol or drugs present for you to have a good time with people, then those aren't the people you want to be hanging out with (1 Corinthians 15:33). Real friends can have a good time together doing the simplest of things.

Lastly, I want to warn you about the pressures to date, kiss, hook up, or just interact with boys in general. High school

Letter #12

dating is often a social hierarchy type thing that will tear you apart if you let it. It can feel like everybody else is dating or having their first kiss, except you. In reality, most people are probably experiencing similar fears. There is no rush. Honor God in your decisions and trust Him with the timing! That goes for relationships and everything else...

Breanne

"I am the LORD your God, who brought you out of Egypt, out of the land of slavery. You shall have no other gods before me."

EXODUS 20:2-3

LETTER #13

Meghan,

If I could write a letter to myself in high school, I would start by asking a question: "Where does your identity come from?" High school me probably would have given the good Christian answer and said, "Jesus!" That would have been partially true because I *did* love Jesus and found some identity in Him. What I *did not* realize though, was that I loved sports and placed my worth in them just as much or even more than my identity in Christ.

What I wish I had known in high school is something I still have to remind myself of today. I wish I'd known things of this world will always try to get our attention and take the throne of our hearts. Once you start letting things take root where they do not belong, you begin to let them define you and your worth. Then, all of a sudden, your identity is being found in sources that cannot give you life and true satisfaction. Additionally, sometimes things that are really important to us can become our idols, and most of the time we don't see it happening (Exodus 20:3). Well, at least I didn't realize it when it happened to me.

Letter #13

It took me learning the hard way and being medically retired from the sport I loved my senior year of high school to realize that I was holding tighter to my identity in a sport than to my identity in Christ. I deceived myself and others saying that I wanted to use basketball to glorify the Lord. While that was partially true, what I was really doing was using basketball for my worth and identity. It wasn't enough for me to be Sydney the Christ-follower. I needed to be Sydney the Christ-follower and the basketball player. I had my first knee reconstruction going into my freshman year of high school. It wasn't until after my fourth knee reconstruction, when the game of basketball was taken from me, that I realized the title "basketball player" was where I found my true identity. When basketball was gone, I didn't know who I was anymore. I didn't know what my purpose in life was, and I was left feeling bitter, broken, depressed, and angry.

It's okay to have aspirations for they can be incredible things used for the Lord's glory. But those aspirations can easily become idols if we allow them to take the throne of our heart and we start seeking them more than we seek the Lord. You might love school and have great grades. You might be extremely talented athletically and be amazing at your sport. You might have an incredible family who loves and supports you. All these things can be awesome, but they are not meant to fulfill you and give you purpose.

John 4:13–14 (ESV) says, "Jesus said to her, 'Everyone who drinks of this water will be thirsty again, but whoever drinks of the water that I will give him will never be thirsty again. The water that I will give him will become in him a spring of water welling up to eternal life.'"

I was constantly thirsty because I was drinking from a well that was bound to run dry. When my injuries came, I was crushed, lost, broken, and angry because my "water" was in the form of athletics. I was confused because in my mind, athletics was what made me worthy, so why would that be taken from me? But I came to realize that's what idols do. They falsely feed the flesh in the same way McDonald's only satisfies us temporarily, but in the long term, they will fail us. However, if we seek our identity and satisfaction in Jesus, we find love, peace, kindness, joy, and more even in the midst of trials. The holy and living water of Jesus is the only thing that can fill our cup and sustain us forever.

That's not to say that life isn't going to be tough sometimes. My knee surgeries were still extremely hard on me. Life can hurt, and there will be trials of many kinds (James 1:2). But those trials are not who we are nor what define us. For us to know our identity, we have to know who Jesus is and what He says about us. He says as children of God we are chosen, redeemed, His special possession, loved, fearfully and wonderfully made, and so many other incredible things (Psalm 139:14; 1 Peter 2:9). But how can I know that if I don't know Him? It is important to dive into His Word so we can get to know Him better and be reminded of the life-giving truth of the Gospel (John 14:6).

God allowed me to be broken so He could reclaim His throne in my life and I could abide in Him and only Him. What I thought was the biggest loss of my life ended up being my biggest gain. Only Jesus can transform like that. I am so grateful that God can use difficult circumstances to turn my focus back to Him. When I lost basketball, I felt like I lost my life, my identity, and my purpose. In reality, losing basketball allowed me to find all of those things and more. God gives and He takes away. He does not take away with evil motives, rather to teach us, to refine us, and to draw us nearer to Him.

"So then, just as you received Christ Jesus as Lord, continue to live your lives in him, rooted and built up in him, strengthened in the faith as you were taught, and overflowing with thankfulness" (Colossians 2:6–7).

Take heart, my friend. Your worth isn't defined by what you do or others' opinions. Your true identity and hope are found in our mighty and merciful God, and nothing can separate you from His love that is in Christ Jesus our Lord (Romans 8:38–39).

Sydney

"So whether you eat or drink or whatever you do, do it all for the glory of God."

1 CORINTHIANS 10:31

LETTER #14

Hi,

If I made a list of all the things I wish I had known in high school it would probably be very long, but I will try to summarize :)

First, looking back I realize I should have been more selective with the people I spent time with. The people you hang around shape who you become, whether you like to admit it or not. They can bring huge amounts of life and joy, or they can cause the biggest wounds. I wish I pursued people who were godly and would've had a more positive influence on me. Instead, I fell into a place of putting pressure on myself to stay loyal to people who didn't appreciate me.

Secondly, enjoy life while glorifying God to the fullest (1 Corinthians 10:31). I wish I would've explored more of what good old-fashioned fun looked like as a teenager. I worked hard throughout high school and felt super independent and responsible in those years. Don't forget to lighten up though, learning who you are through hobbies, music, and quality time with true friends! Enjoy the little moments as you continue the journey of becoming an adult. I hope you can look back on high school and be thankful for every experience, the good and the bad. I wish you the best!

God Bless,

Rachel

"Trust in the LORD with all your heart and lean not on your own understanding; in all your ways submit to him, and he will make your paths straight."

PROVERBS 3:5–6

LETTER #15

Dear High Schooler,

High school is such a fun time full of new adventures, special people, and funny stories that will last a lifetime. Soak it ALL up and dive into the new things God has for you. However, high school also has the paradox of really hard things. There will be too much homework, friend drama, and a new transition into young adulthood as you prepare for college or whatever else may lie ahead. Allow yourself to embrace both these new highs and lows at the same time.

I made the mistake of putting myself in a box of what I thought I wanted and needed to be. In high school, there's this pressure to get it right: What college will I attend? What career do I want? And so much more. For example, I applied to Geneva College in May of my senior year as a joke because my parents didn't think we could afford a private university two hours away. Then, I got a merit scholarship from them, meaning I actually *could* afford to go. I thought I wanted to be a nurse at the time. Despite the scholarship though, I didn't like their nursing program. So, I went to my local RN nursing program in my hometown that fall…and I dropped out two days in!

Luckily, when I called Geneva to ask if I could have my scholarship back and change my major, the doors were still open. I settled into an elementary education and special education degree working with children...quite a drastic turnaround, right? I moved into my dorm *that night* and stayed focused for the next three years. I have loved being a teacher ever since. Could God have worked the other path for my good? Of course He could have, but I listened to that little tug on my heart that compelled me down a different path. God has now used it powerfully as I am beginning a new adventure as a full-time missionary in the Bahamas using my teaching degree. If I had never taken that U-turn, I'm not sure where I would be right now. So allow yourself U-turns, even when they seem impossible. Trust me girl, you don't need to have it all figured out in high school.

Furthermore, invest in your female friendships. When I was in high school I often over-prioritized my dating relationships. My female friends were not as important as they should have been in my life. If your parents approve, nothing is wrong with taking your dating relationship seriously and making it a priority, but sometimes you can get too caught up in it. High school is a unique time to create lifelong friends, especially those of faith. So don't quit activities with your fellow sisters in Christ for a boy. Trust me girly, if he's one worth keeping around, he won't pressure you to give up things that are good for your heart. Wait for him to pursue you. I learned when I was the one doing all the pursuing, he wasn't meant for me.

Lastly, allow yourself space to rest, have fun, and go on adventures. Yes, high school is a big part of setting yourself up for success in the future and you need to take it seriously. Always doing homework 'til 4 am and never having some fun though is not healthy! You won't make it far mentally if you don't rest and do things that fill your soul. I can totally sympathize with the fact that high school can be a lot of work and a super full schedule. Try to plan ahead and stay on top of your homework so you can go to the events/activities when they come up. Those spaces are always where God developed me the most. Trust me, plenty of adulting stuff is waiting for you after high school. Don't be in a rush to grow up.

You got this girl. God has you more than you know during this time. Lean into Him and trust He will catch you. The Lord is strong and mighty, just let Him lead (Psalm 24:8).

Sincerely,

Em

"Look at the birds of the air; they do not sow or reap or store away in barns, and yet your heavenly Father feeds them. Are you not much more valuable than they? Can any one of you by worrying add a single hour to your life?"

MATTHEW 6:26–27

LETTER #16

Dear Meghan,

When I was in high school, I was so focused on perfection. I wanted to be the perfect student, the perfect friend, and the perfect athlete. While it is important to try to be the best version of yourself, I wish I hadn't taken myself so seriously. High school is a time to grow, learn, and make friends. Don't expect yourself to be perfect. For me, striving for perfection only led to worrying about pointless things. God specifically tells us <u>not</u> to worry about anything (Philippians 4:6–7).

In retrospect, the things I spent so much time worrying about in high school (grades, appearance, etc.) are insignificant now. I was so concerned about what other people thought of me. I wish I had realized the only person nitpicking me was myself. In reality, you're spending way more time thinking about yourself than other people are thinking about you. Fear stopped me from doing so many things I wanted to do. I was too afraid to go by myself and try new things. Don't let fear hold you back. Join that club, take that class, and reach out to that person! The things I remember from high school aren't the grades I got or the tests I aced. Looking back on high school, I no longer care what other people thought of me or who was doing what. What

Letter #16

I do remember is the time I spent with my friends, the extracurriculars I did, and the events I attended.

The advice I have for you is this:

1. Don't worry about things you can't control (Matthew 6:27). God loves you and has a plan for you.

2. Don't overly focus on what other people think of you.

3. Find a solid group of friends who lift you up. The people you surround yourself with will influence you greatly.

4. Do your best and don't exclusively focus on your shortcomings. Your future is not determined by one bad grade or small mistake.

5. Step outside of your comfort zone.

6. Don't place your self-worth in external factors. Your value doesn't come from the way you look, other people's opinions, or your accomplishments (1 Peter 3:3–4). Your value comes from God!

High school is such an exciting time—enjoy it!!

♡ *Erin*

"For you created my inmost being; you knit me together in my mother's womb. I praise you because I am fearfully and wonderfully made; your works are wonderful, I know that full well."

PSALM 139:13–14

LETTER #17

Hi Meghan!

Your sister has asked me to share with you some things I wish I'd known in high school. It is such a fun, yet overwhelming time. I am not quite sure where you're at or what you may be going through, but I hope that these words can be an encouragement and comfort in some way!

The best advice I can share with you is to be confident in who God made you to be. As a freshman, I felt so much pressure to be more outgoing and outspoken. I know you don't know me well, but I tend to be more reserved and relaxed. I'm content being a listener rather than one who commands attention. In high school, I thought I had to change who I was or else I wouldn't fit in. I felt insecure if I wasn't always surrounded by friends and busy on the weekends. I soon realized that those beliefs I held were not true.

I had a solid, tight-knit group of friends who I loved. Many of them had these big personalities, which brought me so much laughter and joy. If we all had the same personalities though, there would not have been balance in our friendships. I have come to recognize I brought something to my peers and friends that was very special—a source of steady, reliable support. I was able to listen well and offer empathy. It took some time, but I've come to see God created me this way to be a blessing to others. How it must hurt Him when we feel we must become someone other than who He created us to be (Ephesians 2:10).

Your personality, talents, and gifts are probably different than mine; nevertheless, they come from the same God. Be confident in the person He made you to be! Share your unique gifts with others. There may be a person in your life who needs what you have to give, whether they realize/appreciate it or not.

Enjoy this time—it's a blast!! Your high school years are such an opportunity to grow. Soak up all the godly wisdom others share with you. Have a wonderful year!

With love,

Brooke ♡

"Above all else, guard your heart, for everything you do flows from it."

PROVERBS 4:23

LETTER #18

Sweet Sister in Christ,

I don't pretend to know exactly how you feel about high school or growing up. Everyone's story is different. I can share with you my own story though, in hopes you avoid the mistakes I made and find for yourself the same comfort I personally have received from Christ (2 Corinthians 1:3–4).

As an adult, the Lord has brought me on a long journey of healing my wounded heart. Those wounds started in childhood and then grew out of control during high school. Recently, He has been faithful to weed out roots of pain and bitterness in my heart that developed when I was your age. My hope in sharing this is that you may see these potential dangers where I did not and resist the devil so he will flee from you (James 4:7).

For some backstory: As a little kid, I was always playing pretend family. More often than not I played the mom. I would fantasize about meeting my husband or prince and practice taking care of bunches of "babies" (stuffed animals at the time). As I got older, this innocent desire grew. I watched countless Disney movies then graduated to romantic comedies and novels of all kinds. I was always captivated by the smallest love story in any book.

But you see, real life was nothing like my dream worlds. At five years old, I was rejected by the kid I had a crush on. Silly as it may sound, it began to lock down my heart in ways I couldn't understand at the time. Then at 13, I watched a crush date one of my best friends, again hitting home the idea that I was undesirable and unseen. I started to let people believe I wasn't allowed to date because my heart was so afraid of rejection. By the time I got to high school, I was firmly cast in the role of a goodie-two-shoes, Christian girl.

As I reflect back now, I can clearly see that few of those boys were looking to Christ. Also, none of them were ready to lead me in my faith. In fact, none of us were really ready to care for another person's heart. All of the drama around dating was more like dangerous practice, similar to giving a child a flaming baton on her first day of camp because she claims she's interested in someday joining the circus.

I wish that I had really understood *this* in high school: how to take heart, how to be patient and entrust my desires to the Lord, how to not let my heart grow weary, and how to realize that God was good for not handing me a flaming baton before I was ready. I wish I had clung to these truths. Because instead, I allowed the loneliness to spiral into depression, distrust for the Lord's plan for my life, and eventually into damaging sexual fantasy. I was very focused on guarding the purity of my body, but I neglected to guard the purity of my heart and mind. This led to much pain. I could have avoided a lot of heartache and years of depression if I had guarded my heart and mind better back in high school (Proverbs 4:23).

So please, sweet sister, resist the devil's lies saying you are unseen and unloved. I am not sure for you what specific lies will take root, but weed them out! Resist the temptation to give your heart over to despair and rejection. Do not let bitter roots remain unattended in the garden of your heart and mind. For when they are allowed to grow, I can testify that they choke out your joy and peace in the Lord.

But even in all the brokenness and sin I have experienced, there is hope, for God has been faithful to me! Through the wounds borne by Jesus Christ on the cross I have been healed (Isaiah 53:5). And everything the enemy meant for evil to take me out of the fight, the Lord has turned for good. May God be praised! And may you be comforted by this testimony of God's power. Do not grow weary or lose heart, but rather grow in trust of the Lord. Know that no matter how far you fall or how ugly your heart becomes, His grace is sufficient for you and me.

I want to leave you with some ways to cultivate your heart and mind...

- Rather than spending time fretting about boys or drama, learn who the Lord is, the One who made you and loves you (Isaiah 54:5).

- Combat the lies by replacing them with God's Word.

- Spend time thinking about your true identity in Christ by dwelling on things above, not on earthly things (Colossians 3:2).

- Grow in trust that those who seek first the Kingdom of God will receive all they need to sustain them (Matthew 6:33).

- Have faith and keep hope because Jesus will supply you with all you need out of the riches of His glory.

Be encouraged sweet sister!

All my love in Christ Jesus,

♡ *Mia*

"No, in all these things we are more than conquerors through him who loved us. For I am convinced that neither death nor life, neither angels nor demons, neither the present nor the future, nor any powers, neither height nor depth, nor anything else in all creation, will be able to separate us from the love of God that is in Christ Jesus our Lord."

ROMANS 8:37–39

LETTER #19

Dear High Schooler,

High school is such an exciting time! To answer the question of what I wish I had known in high school, I have a few thoughts:

- The activities, sports, clubs, etc. you choose to get involved in during high school are very important, but they do not define who you are. You should get involved in things you enjoy and help you grow. You'll learn a lot of new skills, challenge yourself, and meet new friends along the way.

- Try new things. High school is a great time to step out of your comfort zone and try something different. Maybe you decide to take a class to learn more about a subject or join a club to get involved in the community. There are many opportunities in high school so take advantage of them! Even if you end up not liking what you tried, at least you gave something new a shot.

I wish you the best!
Sincerely,
Macy

"But seek first his kingdom and his righteousness, and all these things will be given to you as well."

MATTHEW 6:33

LETTER #20

Dear Meghan,

I was so excited when your sister asked me to write you this letter. High school was a very defining time in my life. I learned so much about life, myself, others, and God—more than I ever expected to learn. There are many pieces of advice I could give you, but I want to focus on the most important thing I've learned. It actually took me two years into college to understand it, but once I did, it changed my life:

Don't try to be like other people. Be who God created you to be in Christ (Ephesians 2:10).

You'll feel a lot of tugging in different directions to be like other people, talk like other people, act like other people, dress like other people, and make decisions like other people. But ask yourself: Is this who I really am? Is this truly what I want? Or am I just doing this because I want to feel liked and accepted? I encourage you to seek God first in all situations (Matthew 6:33).

For years, I lived my life for other people because I wanted to fit in and not face rejection. But in the end, it just left me empty and broken. Trying to change yourself for others is exhausting. It's not worth it. With Jesus, however, your security and

Letter #20

identity are rooted in His love—a love that is "wide and long and high and deep" (Ephesians 3:17–19).

So, be who God created you to be in Christ—with all your unique quirks, personality traits, godly passions, and talents. This world does not need more copycats. You have a role in this world and in God's Kingdom to fulfill. Take this life one day at a time, and just enjoy the adventure of discovering who God created you to be and what He created you to do.

Love others deeply along the way (1 Peter 4:8). There is so much brokenness and evil in this world. You have no idea how much of an impact you'll make in others' lives simply by showing them love. They will hopefully see Jesus through your love, and that is one of the greatest gifts you can give them (John 13:34–35).

High school is an important time in your life.
But it is not everything.
The drama won't last, so be encouraged.
Your social status won't last either.
So focus on the things that truly matter—the things that will last.
Your relationship with Jesus.
Your relationships with others.
Your identity and purpose in this life.

High school is an incredible time, and I am so excited for you!

Praying for you,

Mackenzie

"Devote yourselves to prayer, being watchful and thankful."

COLOSSIANS 4:2

LETTER #21

Meghan,

Humility is not self-deprecation or putting yourself down just to make sure you stay humble. Instead, I see humility as allowing God to work through you and doing your best to trust God even when you think you know better. God is God and we are not. You were made in God's image and the fact you are on this earth means you have something unique to offer the world (Genesis 1:27). You are made for so much more than you could even imagine.

You may not feel like you have community or many people to turn to in this time, but know that God is working in ways you can't see. Most importantly, make time for intentional and quiet prayer with just you and God (Colossians 4:2). Close the door and sit with Him; in the silence allow Him to speak.

Daniela

"Yet to all who did receive him, to those who believed in his name, he gave the right to become children of God—children born not of natural descent, nor of human decision or a husband's will, but born of God."

JOHN 1:12–13

LETTER #22

Dear Meghan,

If I could go back, these are the things I would tell myself in high school...

Be Okay with the Ordinary: I've always been an idealist. So, I went into high school with high expectations: I would find the love of my life, earn straight A's, go to so many parties, become homecoming or prom queen, and more. However, not a single one of those things happened. This does not make me a failure or "not good enough." In life, it is worth it and so important to set goals, but if your high school experience does not look like a rendition of *High School Musical*...that's okay. There is nothing wrong with you if you're single, don't take eight million AP classes, aren't popular/prom queen, or don't achieve the very high goals you set. Take it one day at a time and enjoy high school. It goes by fast. Comparing yourself to others will cause you to miss out on the beauty of your own life. Don't fall for this trap! Instead, embrace the unique path God ordained for you before you were even born.

Not Everyone Will Like You: This one was the hardest pill to swallow. I went into high school with a lack of clarity on who

Letter #22

I was and a lack of security in my identity in Christ. This caused me to be swayed by the wind. If someone didn't like me, it was the end of the world. If a boy told me I wasn't beautiful, I wasn't. If a friend did not include me in their plans, I was unimportant. You may meet people who don't see you as valuable as you see them or people who treat you like complete trash. If there's one thing I've learned though, it's that my value is set by Christ, and it doesn't change because of anyone's inability to see it.

It's Okay to Not Be Perfect: Sometimes our teachers, friends, parents, or even we ourselves put unrealistic pressure on us to be the best at what we do. In high school, you may fail a test or two, not do so well in a class, and struggle to balance your extracurricular and academic life. That is <u>okay</u>! Struggling with this does not mean you're a failure, but an imperfect human trying to figure out what works for you. Although they may seem like it, grades and test scores are not the most important thing. I didn't have the best GPA or SAT score, yet I still got into my dream college. My advice is to do your best, participate in activities you're passionate about, and put your faith in God whose plans stand firm forever (Psalm 33:11). Remember, your value is never in your grades. It is in God, who calls you His beloved child when you accept Him into your heart (John 1:12–13).

Be Who God Made You to Be: Don't change who you are just to fit in. High school is the time to discover your interests and see what you may want to pursue long-term. Do not feel pressured if you do not know what you want to do as soon as everyone else does. I came into high school certain I would be a doctor, but as time went on I found myself interested in many other careers such as being a journalist, author, accountant, or dentist. I discovered computer science halfway through my junior year and now couldn't imagine myself doing anything else. Some people are born knowing what they are meant to do, and some don't discover it until halfway through their collegiate career. Whatever your case is, trust God's timing, and do not feel pressured by anyone to know what you want to do. Be sure to keep an open mind about it: take classes that sound interesting to you, do research, and talk to people in a field you are interested in. If there is a career path you feel called to pursue, as long as you've sought God through Scripture, prayer, and wise counsel...do not let anyone hold you back :) (Proverbs 15:22; 2 Timothy 3:16–17).

Relationships: If I could go back, I would tell myself two things: A boy's validation does not determine my worth, and there will be many boys you will meet throughout your life! So, it is not the end of the world if one, two, or even a million boys in high school do not like you. It may seem like the end of the world because when we have a crush on people, we tend to put them on a pedestal and make our lives revolve around them. But the truth is they are just normal people like you, and you will meet many other people in the future. If I put half of the time I spent stressing over boys into working on my hobbies, improving myself, putting effort into school, or building my relationship with God, I would have had much more joy in high school. There is a lot of pressure from social media and friends to get into relationships, but I truly believe high school is the time to get to know yourself better, hone in on your talents, and blossom into the young woman God is molding you to be. But if you do find yourself in a relationship, holding fast to your convictions is imperative. Always know your boundaries and do not let any boy (no matter how cute) cause you to break or even stretch them. If a guy ever tries to force you to do anything or does not respect your boundaries, run and never look back. It will only get worse. Do not settle for less. Trust that God has a plan for you and His timing is always perfect. Whether that plan may look like being single or in a relationship, always rejoice in the Lord (Philippians 4:4).

God Has a Purpose for Your Life: As you walk through the hills and valleys of high school, the most important thing to know is this—God has a good plan for those who love Him (Romans 8:28). It is a plan that is unique and divinely-crafted. As Psalm 139:16 says, "all the days ordained for me were written in your book before one of them came to be." God created you and has a purpose for your life! As you go through high school, walk with your head high. Hold on tightly to God's hand, as He is your source of help and strength. Involve Him in every aspect of your life, pray to Him while you study, ask Him about what classes to take, and make His Kingdom the first priority in every decision (Matthew 6:33). Embrace the person you were made to be and all you have to offer. You are beautiful, fearfully and wonderfully made by God (Psalm 139:14)!

Krystal

"Jesus replied, 'You do not realize now what I am doing, but later you will understand.'"

JOHN 13:7

LETTER #23

Hello, High Schooler!

Looking back on my high school years, I can hardly remember who I was even though in the moment I felt like I had it all figured out. Freshman year, softball was my entire identity and basically the only thing I cared about. I thought everything in life would be great if I made varsity as a freshman. Well, I did, which led to me having multiple bad coaches that squashed my confidence and made me hate the sport (an experience all too many athletes have). It took me years to realize if I hadn't had this negative experience with what I thought was the most important thing in life, I would have never started playing tennis my sophomore year of high school. If I had never started playing tennis, I would have never attended Grove City College to play on their team. I would have never had the opportunity to be a graduate assistant at a university after college and receive a free master's degree.

I tell this story because often the older you get, the clearer God's plan becomes. There are times you are able to look back on your past and understand more clearly why God orchestrated things the way He did. You might not be able to see it in the moment, but have faith that closed doors in athletics, social groups, fine arts, academics, etc. may be part of a bigger plan.

Janine

"Don't be deceived, my dear brothers and sisters. Every good and perfect gift is from above, coming down from the Father of the heavenly lights, who does not change like shifting shadows."

JAMES 1:16–17

LETTER #24

Dear High Schooler,

I wish I had learned sooner that our Father God delights in giving good gifts. And give abundantly He does! Recently, Matthew 7:7–11 has been on my heart; it reads, "Ask and it will be given to you; seek and you will find; knock and the door will be opened to you. For everyone who asks receives; the one who seeks finds; and to the one who knocks, the door will be opened. Which of you, if your son asks for bread, will give him a stone? Or if he asks for a fish, will give him a snake? If you, then, though you are evil, know how to give good gifts to your children, how much more will your Father in heaven give good gifts to those who ask him!"

My view of God radically changed when I finally embraced the knowledge that He longs to bless me out of love, not because I've finally checked off my ultra-spiritual to-do list—spending hours in prayer, fasting, service, etc. How arrogant to even assume I could earn His blessing! While all of those things are laudable, they should stem from a heart so in love with God it can't help but respond, not one resentful of burdensome expectations. There is so much freedom in boldly approaching the Throne of Grace, knowing that in the Lord's presence we are offered true peace and hope.

Emily

"Therefore go and make disciples of all nations, baptizing them in the name of the Father and of the Son and of the Holy Spirit, and teaching them to obey everything I have commanded you. And surely I am with you always, to the very end of the age."

MATTHEW 28:19–20

LETTER #25

Dear Meghan ♡,

I am so thankful to have the opportunity to write you a letter about what I wish I had known in high school! To answer that question, I have quite a bit to say. One of my main takeaways is to treat high school not as something to get over with, but as a time to learn new things, develop skills, and build relationships. Not only will this be helpful when your time in high school is over, but it'll also help you really treasure and see God in the present moment.

This applies to relationships with teachers as well. I regret not taking classes as seriously as I could have and failing to truly build connections with my teachers. Seeing teachers, bosses, etc. as people, not just their titles, is really important for serving and loving others and just being a responsible adult. Caring about your classes and teachers might even turn into an opportunity to proclaim the Gospel to them!

In regard to classmates, I recommend interacting with them early on. As an awkward person myself, it can be hard for me to reach out to people. Looking back, I wish I had reached out before they formed their own groups. Relationships with classmates are great to have, and it's a good way to practice being there for others and loving them well. I also recommend joining a club even if you're not skilled at it (e.g. sports, music, debate, or dance) because these things take practice, which matters more than talent.

Most of all, I wish I had known Jesus! I wish I had realized the incredible sacrifice He made on the cross in order to pay the price for our sins. 1 John 4:10 says, "This is love: not that we loved God, but that he loved us and sent his Son as an atoning sacrifice for our sins." Praise the Lord! What an amazing God! It is such a joy to know His love and have His Spirit. Jesus enriches every experience, whether joy or struggle, far beyond what we can do on our own.

Love, your sister in Christ,

Kailyn ♡

"You are the light of the world. A town built on a hill cannot be hidden. Neither do people light a lamp and put it under a bowl. Instead they put it on its stand, and it gives light to everyone in the house. In the same way, let your light shine before others, that they may see your good deeds and glorify your Father in heaven."

MATTHEW 5:14–16

LETTER #26

Dear Meghan,

High school is a very exciting time in life, and you are going to learn so much about yourself. Although there are many things I want to write to you, there is one very important lesson that I learned in high school that I hope you can take away from this letter…

No matter what goal you're striving to accomplish, embrace the friendships and the time with family during the journey. The memories you make on the way to the finish line are priceless and will be what you look back on and value. You won't look back in 10 years and cherish the trophy you won at state, the perfect test score you made in a difficult class, being nominated as homecoming queen, or being named an all-state athlete. You'll look back and cherish the meaningful times with the people you loved, and the moments you were able to shine the light of Christ to those in need.

I'm grateful for my high school experience because it taught me to enjoy the *journey* to the finish line, not just the finish line itself. I was an aspiring Division I golfer with the goal of being a professional athlete. I worked relentlessly during my four years of high school to achieve those goals, and I'm grateful that the Lord allowed me to accomplish them eventually. I want you to know though, once you achieve that amazing goal you are striving for, you very well may not have that "I've finally made it!" moment. I was shocked and slightly disappointed when I wasn't as happy as I imagined I would be when I finally reached the finish line of my goal. In high school, I viewed happiness as a destination and forgot life was happening in the current moment. I was so lasered in on my goal, I forgot to be grateful in the present moment and cherish the time I had with the people around me.

I remember I would so often miss the football game, the sleepover, or the family get together on the weekend because I thought I had to sacrifice all those things to be successful in my sport. It's not true. Working your hardest is very important, and I encourage you to be disciplined. I hope you remember though, as you strive toward your goal, enjoy those little moments you have with the people you love. I've learned that life is about the journey, not just the destination. Be grateful and enjoy every day the Lord has given you.

Julia

"For I am not ashamed of the gospel, because it is the power of God that brings salvation to everyone who believes: first to the Jew, then to the Gentile."

ROMANS 1:16

LETTER #27

Dear High Schooler,

High school can be a great time in life and bring so much growth. Nobody has it all figured out and that is okay! Here are some things I have learned over the past four years while I was in high school. I hope these words are helpful to you as you go on your journey!

In high school, I often changed myself in subtle ways to fit into the crowd and not seem different. I think it is just a natural human instinct to avoid standing out and going against the flow. I would act differently at school than I would at home or church because of the people I was around and influenced by. It was almost like I was ashamed of being a Christian…

I regret shrinking down in my faith because of the fear of what others may have thought of me for being an outspoken Christian (Galatians 1:10). Jesus says in John 15:18, "If the world hates you, keep in mind that it hated me first." When we are obedient in living sold out for Christ, we don't need to be overly concerned about the opinions of those around us because the Lord promises to walk with us! I wish I had realized other people's opinions of me don't determine my worth and identity. Instead, my worth and identity are found in Jesus Christ.

Letter #27

Another thing I wish I had known in high school is that reading my Bible and investing my free time in other activities/hobbies are way healthier than scrolling my day away on social media. As I was trying to figure out who I was and what to place my identity in, social media quickly took up lots of my time. This led to insecurity, comparison, and filling my mind with the opinions and lies of the world rather than the truth of what God thought of me.

The world says we need to look a certain way, but God says we are fearfully and wonderfully made (Psalm 139:14). God created us in His own image and knows the number of hairs on our head (Genesis 1:27; Luke 12:6–7). He loves us so deeply and way more than any human on this earth could (Ephesians 3:17–19). Breaking off the lies of the enemy that hold us captive and living out the truth of God brings true restoration and freedom!

Always remember, the One who created you loves you most!

Kirsten ♡

"Cast all your anxiety on him because he cares for you. Be alert and of sober mind. Your enemy the devil prowls around like a roaring lion looking for someone to devour."

1 PETER 5:7–8

LETTER #28

Meghan,

In high school, there were times I didn't know if or how I would get through. Every single year I would worry that the plethora of assignments I was given would be too much, and I wouldn't be able to complete them all. But with time, as I did the little I could do, piece by piece, I saw that I was going to ride this insurmountable wave even if I got tossed and knocked around. Worry is a sad part of life. The Apostle Paul calls us to give everything to God in prayer though. Philippians 4:6–7 (ESV) says:

> Do not be anxious about anything, but in everything by prayer and supplication with thanksgiving let your requests be made known to God. And the peace of God, which surpasses all understanding, will guard your hearts and your minds in Christ Jesus.

Christians often put prayer as their last resort. Our minds are frequently riddled with the worst possible outcomes. A pastor at my church once said, "Worry is like a rocking chair. It'll give you something to do, but won't get you anywhere." I wasted so much time worrying about what I couldn't do that I failed to spend enough time on what I needed to. So, as you go through high school, I encourage you to worry less and pray more. Bring your requests to God in prayer, and always remember to give thanks.

Ese

"If we claim to be without sin, we deceive ourselves and the truth is not in us. If we confess our sins, he is faithful and just and will forgive us our sins and purify us from all unrighteousness."

1 JOHN 1:8–9

LETTER #29

Meghan!

High school is quite a journey! It is full of amazing moments and hard moments. But don't be discouraged because every year you will grow and mature. Having gone through high school, I want to leave you with some advice:

1. Stay true to what you believe. Temptations, drama, and stress can certainly cause you to blur your character.
2. School definitely gets harder. But don't be scared because you learn a lot as you are challenged academically. If you're struggling, don't be afraid to reach out to your teachers! They are there to help you!
3. You're not going to be perfect. We are all human and fall into sin (Romans 3:23). But know, when you give your heart over to Jesus and confess your sins, He will forgive you and purify you of all unrighteousness (1 John 1:9).
4. People change and friends change. The friend group you had in the past may not be the friend group you have now. That is totally okay!
5. High school flies by. Enjoy it as much as you can :)
6. Trust in the Lord (Proverbs 3:5). I struggled with this a lot through high school. What really helped me was when my

Letter #29

friends and I started a Bible study. That was so necessary and crucial for my faith!

7. As an underclassman, I hope you become friends with upperclassmen who will not only mentor/help you but also shine the light of God in your life! Then, when you become an upperclassman, turn around and do the same for the younger girls.
8. Be kind to everyone, even when people are rude, sassy, or mean. Do/say the little things that can make someone's day. Say hi to random people in the hallways, greet teachers, sit with someone who is by themselves, etc. I missed these opportunities because I was too focused on fitting in!
9. Get involved in your school. I think this is the best way to meet people. Whether it is through clubs, sports, or musicals, it's incredible the people you will meet along the way...
10. Remember, the Lord's presence is <u>ALWAYS</u> with you and you're never alone (Joshua 1:9; Psalm 139:6–10). Even when you can't feel Him or you are in the lowest place, lean on Him. In fact, that is when you should lean on Him most!
11. I forgot about this: DON'T LET A BOY RUIN YOUR FRIENDSHIPS!

Blessings,

Megan

"I will instruct you and teach you in the way you should go; I will counsel you with my loving eye on you."

PSALM 32:8

LETTER #30

Dear Meghan,

I went into high school as a very quiet kid. I struggled to feel confident in the classroom and in my sport. (I was on the sailing team.) As time went on though, I stopped comparing myself to others and saw God's ability to work through the people supporting me. Realizing the truth that God made us and we are His slowly built up my confidence (Psalm 100:3).

I saw the comfort others received when they leaned on God, and this led to my faith being deepened. It was clear, His love grounded them in the waves of life, and He guided them through hard decisions. Though there are always many decisions in front of us, as I look back on life I firmly believe in God's sovereign plan for those who love Him (Romans 8:28). He instructs us in the way we should go, and there is no better place to be than in His will (Psalm 32:8). I tend to overthink, but knowing the truth that God's ways are better than my own is very comforting.

As you navigate high school, always remember the words of Ephesians 2:10, "For we are God's handiwork, created in Christ Jesus to do good works, which God prepared in advance for us to do."

Jen

"Your beauty should not come from outward adornment, such as elaborate hairstyles and the wearing of gold jewelry or fine clothes. Rather, it should be that of your inner self, the unfading beauty of a gentle and quiet spirit, which is of great worth in God's sight."

1 PETER 3:3–4

LETTER #31

Dear High School Self,

After growing up an avid fan of the *High School Musical* series and DCOMs (Disney Channel Original Movies), I had a vision of what high school was going to be like...and let me tell you, much to the chagrin of my third-grade self, it was nothing like I thought it would be. And that is okay! In most situations, even if it does not live up to your expectations, there are positives. As I reflect on my time in high school, there are many things I wish I had known. Below are a few:

1. The little things that feel so big and important right now will not be in the grand scheme of things. Yes, there are exceptions to the rule; however, years down the road it will be inconsequential if your hair looked frizzy this morning, if you got an 88 on the most recent math test as opposed to a 98, or if your crush likes someone else. Life is hard, and your feelings are real, so real...but try to remember that your feelings are just that...feelings. Don't let them call the shots or blind you to all the beauty in front of you.

2. Don't take for granted this time with your family. They are your automatic support system. You will never be a high schooler again, your parents will never be this age again,

and soon enough you will be out of the house. So don't take for granted family dinners, car rides with your parents, movie nights, and all the little things that might feel small now, but truly are important.

3. This world often sends the message that there is a correct timeline that you have to follow. There is so much pressure on teenagers to do this by a certain age, try that by a certain age, look like this by a certain age...and it is SO damaging. Don't allow your friends to pressure you into having your first kiss, your first date, your first boyfriend. Good for you if you never sneak out of the house or don't have wild nights that you can't remember (1 Peter 4:2–5). I know it is easier said than done, but it is so important to stick to your values and morals. It will serve you well in the long run and will be oh-so worth it...

4. Piggybacking off the above sentiments, it is okay to look your age :) Also, it takes a while to grow into your looks sometimes. It can be a challenge to figure out how to best style your hair, put on makeup, find clothes that fit who you are, etc. We now live in a society where 15-year-old girls look like 25-year-old women. People seem to be growing up so quickly...and I think it is harmful. Enjoy where you're at right now in life, while realizing that you will change and grow. Most of all, please know that your beauty doesn't come from outward appearance (1 Peter 3:3–4).

5. Be intentional about the content you consume on social media because it will affect you, your energy, and the way

Letters to High School Girls

you look at yourself/the world around you. In an age where almost anything is at the tip of your fingers, be careful what you spend time doing and looking at. We are what we consume.

6. Some friends are forever and some are for a season, but I would like to think that they all come into our lives for a reason. So, try to learn from these friendships and experiences.

7. High school is not the be all, end all. Be present and try to focus on the positives (no matter how small or big they may be). Realize that this season in your life will eventually come to an end, and there will be things (believe it or not) that you might miss about this time.

8. Comparison is the thief of joy and breeds discontentment. Remember (and here comes the broken record), there is no correct timeline, no correct way to look, and no perfect friendship or dating relationship (even if it might look that way on social media)…

9. Lastly, God works in the most mysterious and beautiful ways. He is with us wherever we go, and He is the One in control; this brings hope and peace that is so powerful (Joshua 1:9). Take life as it comes and enjoy the little moments :)

Love,

Danielle

"Rejoice always, pray continually, give thanks in all circumstances; for this is God's will for you in Christ Jesus."

1 THESSALONIANS 5:16–18

LETTER #32

Dear Meghan,

When I was in high school I wish someone had told me to live in the present. I spent so much of my high school experience working to get into a good college. I paid attention in class, did my homework, studied for tests, and got good grades. I joined a bunch of activities and clubs I didn't truly care about just to add more things to my resume. I skipped so many events for soccer games because I wanted to get recruited. I did everything to ensure that my life after high school would fit the dream I had.

Although none of these things were necessarily bad, looking back, I see they caused me to make a lot of decisions I regret today. For many people, high school is the last four years you spend at home with your family. High school is the time you can pick up hobbies and discover what you like and what you don't. It is the time you can build friendships for life and discover what it means to be a good friend. It is the time when you can find good mentors. It is the time when you can deepen your faith in God and figure out what you believe.

My advice is to take every day as the gift that it is. It is important to plan for the future, but don't let that consume your life. Live

Letter #32

in the moment, experience every day. Journal and record these moments so you can look back and be grateful. Pick up new hobbies, meet new people, and cherish the time with your friends/family. Embrace all that high school brings. Most of all, become firm in your identity and what you stand for. You've got this!

With love,

Mo

"Charm is deceptive, and beauty is fleeting; but a woman who fears the LORD is to be praised."

PROVERBS 31:30

LETTER #33

Dear Meghan,

If I could go back in time and tell my high school self a few things, I would tell her...

1. Outer beauty fades (Proverbs 31:30). Inner beauty brightens. Instead of focusing on being physically attractive or looking put together, cultivate the things people don't always see on the surface—love, joy, peace, patience, kindness, goodness, faithfulness, gentleness, and self-control (Galatians 5:22–23; 1 Peter 3:3–4).

2. Focus on your God-given passions and continue to get better at them. Some of my greatest passions in life include music, growing in my faith, and developing friendships. In retrospect, I wish I had kept those passions more in my focus as a high schooler.

3. Love others without expecting anything in return. Learning how to love selflessly is one of the most beautiful gifts God has given us (Romans 12:10). When we pour into others, we receive the joy of knowing we have served someone else.

4. Hard work is important, but perfectionism and fear of failure are toxic. Pursue academic excellence, but don't be afraid of less than perfect scores. Life is more than grades, and I've learned the most in classes where I've experienced the most failure.

Grow where you're planted girl!

Ellie ♡

"'For my thoughts are not your thoughts, neither are your ways my ways,' declares the LORD. 'As the heavens are higher than the earth, so are my ways higher than your ways and my thoughts than your thoughts.'"

ISAIAH 55:8–9

LETTER #34

Dear Meghan,

Here are 10 things I've learned since high school...

1. Be content no matter the circumstances.

Let's face it: Life's hard sometimes! It's so easy to complain and wish for things to be different. But the reality is we live in a broken world. There are a lot of things we don't have any control over. What we do have more control over is how we respond to what's going on around us. Will we blame our circumstances or take responsibility for how we react to them? Will we be content or complain? Paul, in Philippians 4:11–13, tells us the key to being content:

> I am not saying this because I am in need, for I have learned to be content whatever the circumstances. I know what it is to be in need, and I know what it is to have plenty. I have learned the secret of being content in any and every situation, whether well fed or hungry, whether living in plenty or in want. I can do all this through him who gives me strength.

2. Be confident in who God made you to be.

I haven't always been the most confident girl. I played basketball but would rarely shoot in games because I didn't want to mess up. In reality, I was a decent shooter, and I would have only gotten better if I had taken more shots. Also, I'm a bit weird and sometimes shy. In high school, I let this define me. I was quiet and didn't talk to many people. I didn't know what to say and was afraid I'd be awkward. More than worrying about what others thought of me, looking back, I should have focused more of my attention on being like Christ and who He made me to be. Let Him shine through you!

3. Life may not turn out as you planned and that's ok.

High school Emily thought for sure she'd be married by now and probably have a couple kids. Not gonna lie, I've cried about this a time or two (or more). Ever since I was little, I wanted "a little farm and a yard full of kids" in the words of Kenny Chesney. That hasn't happened yet, and that's ok. I've been learning to be content where God has me and to trust His timing. One of my friends told me, "God may be using you in ways He couldn't if you were married." What an encouragement that was to fully embrace where I am right now and make the most of the opportunities God gives me! It is true, being single does provide a special opportunity to have undivided devotion to the Lord (1 Corinthians 7:34–35).

4. Don't compromise your values for friendships and especially not for boys.

Ugh. I cannot stress this one enough! I've been there more than once. It's a scary place to be. I let my desire to be liked and please others become more important than sticking to my values and pleasing God. In one instance, it was dating a guy who wasn't a Christian. At first, I told him I couldn't date him, but then I kept talking to him and fell in love. I told myself, "Well, maybe it's ok, as long as I don't marry him while he's not a Christian." I just set myself up for heartbreak. The other situation was compromising my sexual boundaries in a different relationship. I didn't ever have sex, but I let things go farther than I was comfortable. The Bible says there is to be not even a hint of sexual immorality and to flee from it (1 Corinthians 6:18; Ephesians 5:3). Instead of fleeing, I was flirting with it, and it terrified me. Hear me on this: If a boy wants you to compromise your values and God's values, he is definitely not the one for you. Don't even entertain the idea. Kindly and firmly say no, and wait for a man who seeks God with his whole heart. I haven't found him yet, but I'm positive that if it is in God's plan, he will be well worth the wait. I promise you that! Hold tight to your values, and trust in God's faithfulness (Psalm 33:4).

5. Don't be afraid to be the friend who reaches out.

Life gets busy, and time passes quickly. Be the friend you want to have. Reach out to your friends often. I used to think, "Maybe they don't like me. Maybe I'm annoying. If they don't have time for me, they're not real friends." A mindset like this is pretty selfish. I was focused more on myself and how I felt in the friendship. God calls us though to do nothing out of selfish ambition and to put others above ourselves (Philippians 2:3). By reaching out, you can be such an encouragement to your friends. It means the world to me when one of my friends randomly texts me just to check in. I try to do the same by sending a text, writing a card (who doesn't love getting snail mail?), or asking someone to hang out.

6. Embrace your weirdness—everyone's a little weird!

This one builds on being confident in who God made you to be. Everyone has certain quirks they're a little embarrassed about and things they try to keep hidden from people they want to impress. Everyone's unique, and everyone's a little weird. But guess what? I really don't think about other people's weirdness. You're probably the one who notices your weirdness the most. Embrace it and move on. Don't let your perception of other people's opinion of you change who you are. (Now, I'm definitely not saying it's ok to be rude, arrogant, or prideful though.)

7. Be intentional.

Cliché I know, but time flies. Before you know it, you'll be coming up on your 10-year high school reunion. Learn to be intentional with your time, your friendships, your relationships, your actions, and your words. It's so easy to get into a routine and go through the motions of life. Make time for what and who is important to you. Spend your time wisely. Also, be intentional in what you say. Words are very powerful and can build up or tear down. The Bible says the tongue has the power of life and death (Proverbs 18:21). Be mindful of that when you speak, whether you are angry, sad, happy, excited, or joking. Your words matter. How you live matters. Be intentional.

8. Do challenging things—they're well worth it.

Just do it! Want to climb Mt. Everest? Do it. Want to run a marathon? Do it. Want to work while going to college? Do it. Want to read the Bible in a year? Do it. But don't rely on motivation to get you through. You must develop self-discipline. For example, if I only went running when I was motivated, there is no way I would have ever run a marathon. I had to develop self-discipline so that when I wasn't feeling it, I would do it anyway. Never be afraid to do something simply because it's challenging. Make achievable goals, create a plan, and stick to it even when you don't feel like it. Self-discipline will get you far in life. Completing hard things can build character and often draws me closer to God. I'd say the benefits are well worth enduring the hard moments.

9. Don't make excuses.

Excuses are so easy to make: "I'm too tired, too busy, too sad, too lazy, too stressed." The list goes on. Excuses hold you back. Have someone keep you accountable. Share your goals with others so they can check in on you. Also, don't make excuses for your actions. "I was mad, hungry, tired..." Excuses play the blame game. Own up to your mistakes, and move on. You are responsible for how you act, no matter how you feel.

10. Never be afraid or ashamed to reach out for help when you are struggling.

I have gone through some struggles alone because I was too ashamed of my poor choices to seek help from wise counsel. I thought for sure if I reached out they'd be ashamed of me too. One time I dated someone I knew I shouldn't have (as I mentioned previously). I really liked him, but he wasn't a Christian and we didn't share the same values. I knew it wasn't wise, and the Bible warns against it (2 Corinthians 6:14). I also knew I should talk about it to people I trusted and seek wise counsel (Proverbs 15:22). However...I kept it to myself. When we broke up, I hurt so much. I kept that to myself too. I knew the hurt was from my own wrongdoing because I chose to ignore God. It took a long time to heal from that because I was too ashamed to reach out and seek help from godly mentors. Please reach out! The truth is we all struggle in some capacity, and God didn't intend for us to fight through it alone. He gives us His Spirit, His Word, and His people to lovingly guide us through life—the ups, the downs, and the in-betweens.

Some of these lessons overlap a bit. Some I'm still learning. I have a feeling it's a lifelong process, but I'm so happy to share them with you. My prayer is that you will be able to learn from me and not make some of the same mistakes I've made.

So much love for you, sweet girl!

Emily

"And I pray that you, being rooted and established in love, may have power, together with all the Lord's holy people, to grasp how wide and long and high and deep is the love of Christ, and to know this love that surpasses knowledge—that you may be filled to the measure of all the fullness of God."

EPHESIANS 3:17–19

LETTER #35

Hi Meghan,

You are doing so, so well. You're working hard, you're kind, you're faithful. You're going to change so much during these high school years. It will feel weird, frustrating, and really hard sometimes. You might have days where you wish something about your body looked different. I've been there too. Remember, your true identity and who you are is unchanging in Christ.

Also, let yourself be unique. So many people around you will want to change themselves to fit the world's standards or expectations. At the end of the day when the lights cut off, so many people will have boxed themselves into mimicries of one another…but you will be able to recognize who you are in Christ.

So, I pray you dive into this time of your life knowing you are made by a great God for a great purpose…and you are so deeply loved in Jesus (Ephesians 2:10; Ephesians 3:17–19).

I know your sister loves you so much and that an entire community filled with women of God are rooting for you.

Rachel

"One who has unreliable friends soon comes to ruin, but there is a friend who sticks closer than a brother."

PROVERBS 18:24

LETTER #36

Dear High Schooler,

Find the people who build you up and encourage you. Stick by those friends, even if you don't have every single thing in common with them. Connection without convenience is a true indicator of friendship. You will have friends that come naturally through similar class schedules or sports teams. Utilize those spaces to make friends, but don't pass up the opportunity to get to know those without shared experiences, even if it takes going out of your way to get to know them. The friends from high school that I've stayed closest with after graduation are the ones who made an effort to spend time with me while in high school. Proximity was never what brought us together...it was the connection and truly knowing each other that did.

Natalie

"Now to him who is able to do immeasurably more than all we ask or imagine, according to his power that is at work within us, to him be glory in the church and in Christ Jesus throughout all generations, for ever and ever! Amen."

EPHESIANS 3:20–21

LETTER #37

Dear Meghan,

I love you so much and I am so proud to be your sister! High school is such a special time. I have lots of happy memories at BPHS! Looking back though, there are a few things I wish I had known...

For much of high school, I put my self-worth and identity in things of this world: sports, my physical appearance, guys' opinions of me, grades, etc. As you saw firsthand, this led me to live on a constant emotional rollercoaster. If I did well at practice one day I would be elated, and if I did poorly I would be crushed. It was a constant fluctuation between ups and downs, highs and lows. (I know this made things hard on you all at home too.) I worked endlessly to earn the approval of others I so desperately craved. With that came crippling fear and anxiety because I was always striving to measure up and prove I was a "somebody."

As you know though, in my senior year, I encountered someone who had the power to give me freedom from this pressure and a peace that surpassed understanding. His name is Jesus :) In Him is where our true identity and worth are found. He loved us so much that He died to pay the price for our sins (1 John 4:9–10)!

Letter #37

That is a crazy, incredible love, better than anything this world could ever give us. It's a love that doesn't fluctuate, but instead is steadfast ♡ (Lamentations 3:22–23).

Something else about Jesus that has stuck out to me recently is we don't have to earn His love and salvation. In fact, we can't! Ephesians 2:8–9 says, "For it is by grace you have been saved, through faith—and this is not from yourselves, it is the gift of God—not by works, so that no one can boast." It is finished. We have been saved by the sacrifice of Christ (John 19:30)! I sometimes forget this, but our gift of a relationship with Christ is the one thing that will satisfy our deepest desires forever. Don't waste energy on the emotional roller coaster trying to earn validation from guys, your appearance, soccer, academics, etc. Those things will only fill you momentarily anyway and are nothing compared to the fulfillment found in Christ. The exhausting race for human approval is needed no more. We can live freely and joyfully for an audience of One!

There are lots of other things I wish I had known in high school, but that's the main one so I'll leave it at that. If you need anything, you know where to find me! Don't forget, your identity is in Jesus and that changes everything...

With love,

Kelsey

ACKNOWLEDGEMENTS

To my friends who wrote these letters: I have witnessed firsthand and been blessed by your godly wisdom over the years. It brings me such joy to pass some of that wisdom on to the girls following behind us. You are the backbone of this book.

To my brothers and sisters in Christ who have come alongside me in this endeavor: Your contributions are far too many to name individually. Thank you for being willing to share your talents, wisdom, and knowledge. From checking Bible citations to answering "just a couple quick questions," it was a true team effort and a picture of what 1 Corinthians 12 describes as the Body of Christ.

To my family: Your unwavering confidence in me through my (sometimes unconventional) life pursuits has been such a blessing. In both the highs and the lows, your support has always been a constant. I am grateful for you.

To my sister, Meghan: How crazy is it that one question you asked me five years ago turned into this? That is what God does, though—abundantly more than all we can ask or imagine through His power within us (Ephesians 3:20). May you now pass along what *you* wish you had known to the girls behind you.

Most importantly, to the Lord: It is from You, through You, and for You that this book has come to completion (Romans 11:36). I pray it brings honor to Your Name.

Made in the USA
Monee, IL
09 February 2025